The Ralph STEADman BOOK OF CATS

For information about permission to reproduce selections from this book, write to Permissions, Houghton Mifflin Harcourt Publishing Company, 215 Park Avenue South, New York, New York 10003.

www.hmhbooks.com

First published in Great Britain in 2012 by Atlantic Books

Library of Congress Cataloging-in-Publication Data is available.
ISBN 978-0-547-59400-2

Printed in China
SCP 10 9 8 7 6 5 4 3 2 1

The Ralph STEADman

BooK of

CATS

HOUGHTON MIFFLIN HARCOURT

BOSTON   NEW YORK

2012

CATS

I am trying to figure out if I like cats, not whether I adore them, love them –
even admire them – but whether I can tolerate them at all. But I don't want to
appear even to dwell on the subject.

The first cat I actually owned was called Tishy, because it rhymes with 'fishy'. Many people have a phobia about cats. They are known as ailurophobes. Believe it or not, many famous world leaders – usually dictators – feared cats. Ghengis Khan loathed them, as did Alexander the Great – which, of course, rhymes with hate. And logically – if we continue down this route – Hitler couldn't stand the sight of cat shit; not a bit of it! And I don't blame him. It's the only thing that showed his human side!

Phobias are deeper feelings than 'dislikes' and can cause sweating and palpitations, nausea, lack of breath and a dry mouth.

The Cat that wanted to be a MOUSE!

That is a horrible condition to suffer simply because you happen not to like damn cats! They cannot help being cuddly things that wrap themselves around your ankles, because they want to be stroked and made a fuss of, but that is why people get the creeps and wonder what else they want. They don't want anything else. But they don't want to give you anything either! They are smug; they never contribute a goddamn thing to the world and they just want feeding for free. If a cat 'adopts' you, it is a kind of curse. You are supposed to feel grateful because, in a sort of way, they will clean you out of rodents. This they are good at, and they carry out that odious task like slaves, though they are fulfilling a deep craving of their own, so NEVER feel sorry for them; I don't! It is all for them. This soft, purring mammal is probably the single most self-centred beast in all of nature and that is probably why they give us the creeps!

GONE PUSSY

Ralph STEADman

WHITE PUSSYFOOTING

Ralph STEADman 2.90.

CAT LINES

Ralph STEADman 2013

CATART

Ralph STEADman 20.

No.1. The MOUSER

First in a series
of violent cartoons
for children

Ralph STEADman 77

NEVER MIND MY TAIL— LOOK TO THE FUTURE!!
CAT PHILOSOPHY..
Ralph STEADman

RURAL SCENE   Ralph STEADman 2010.

CAT LAUGHING AT SOME KING OR OTHER
PROBABLY — KING LUDD !!

Ralph STEADman 290

ARCH BUDDIES

Ralph STEADman 2010

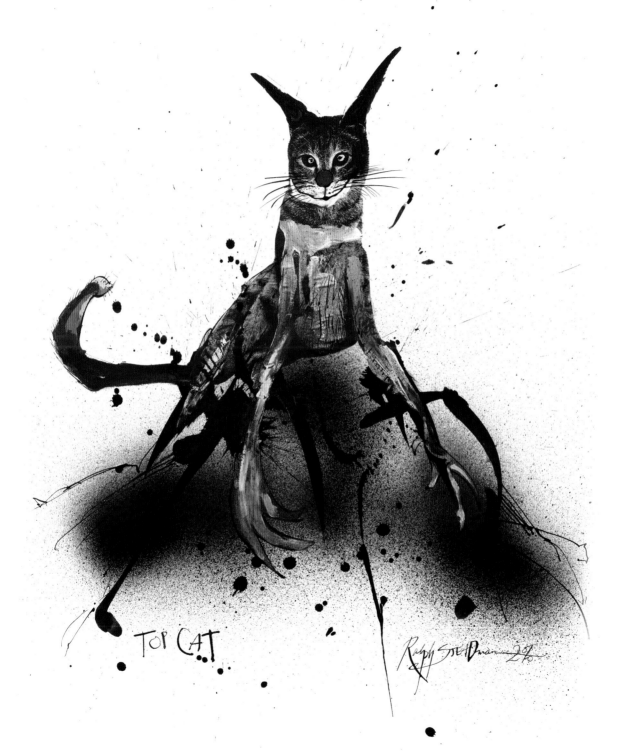

TOP CAT

Ralph STEADMAN 2/

THE EDITOR'S CAT—TWIGLET. Ralph STEADman 201.

I HAVE A TATTOO FROM MY OWNER HELP!!

A TAIL of TWO CATS!

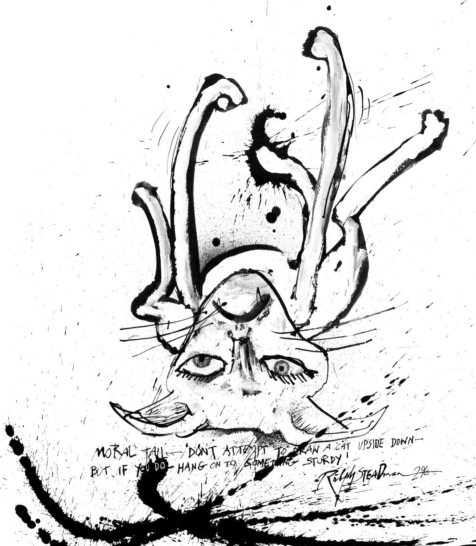

MORAL TAIL — 'DON'T ATTEMPT TO DRAW A CAT UPSIDE DOWN —
BUT IF YOU DO — HANG ON TO SOMETHING STURDY!

Ralph STEADman

DRAT!!

CATALOGUE

CATWALK

Ralph STEADman 2010

CATASTROPHE!

Ralph STEADman 2010

CATLIKE

Ralph STEADman 2010

A VICTIM OF DISTORTION
—ALL 'IT NEEDS IS LOVE!

EVEN FATTERCAT SAT ON THE MAT

CATS ARE THEMSELVES Ralph Steadman 2010

SILLY CATS? DON'T YOU BELIEVE IT!

Ralph STEADman 290

ISIS
IS CAT.
with BOOK OF JONES
which is a BOOK about
ONE CAT.

To ISIS

Ralph STEADman 2010

CAT LIKE

SORT OF...

Ralph STEADman 290

SCHIZOPHRENIC CAT. Ralph STEADman 2010.

CATASTROPHE!

RECLINING MEW   Ralph Steadman 290

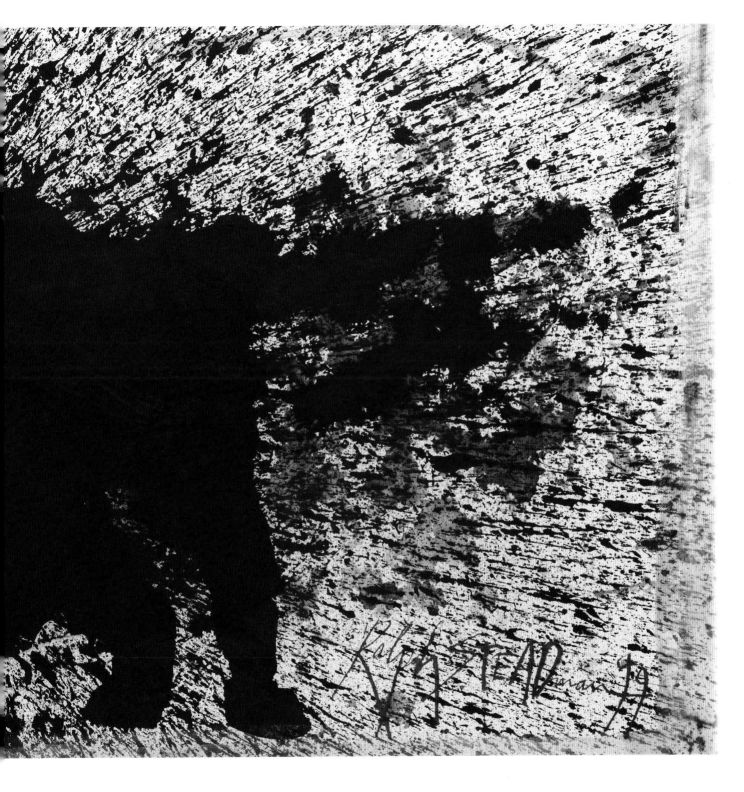

NOT HIS MOTHER!

MY KIND OF CAT

CATFISH

PRANCING CAT

PORTRAIT
OF
TWILLER

FAT
CAT-39

Ralph STEADman 2 90

FAT CAT-1   Ralph STEADman 2010

CAT MESS-1.

Ralph STEADman 2010

CAT GOD FOLLOWERS.

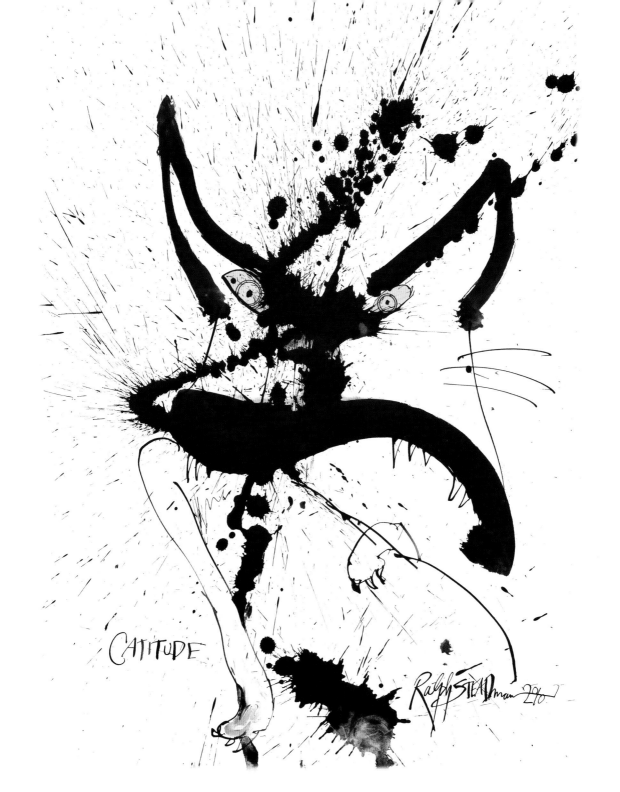

CATITUDE

Ralph STEADman 2010

SEÑOR CAT

Ralph Steadman

CATHARTIC.

Ralph STEADman 2010.

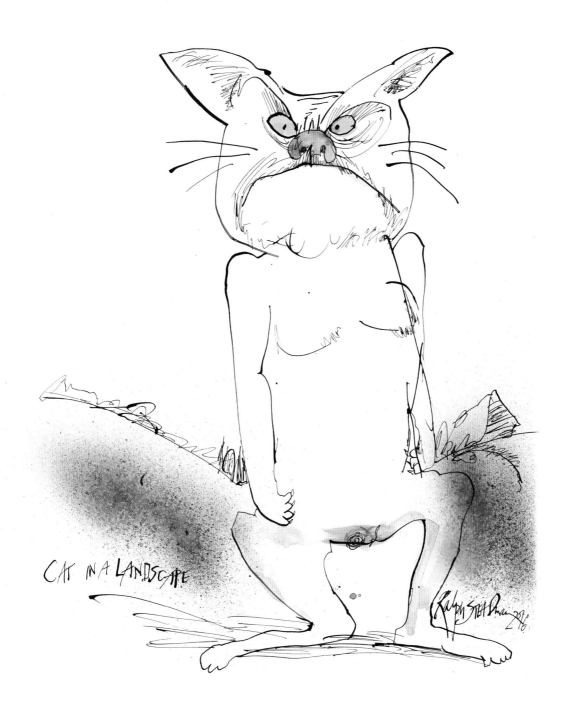

CAT IN A LANDSCAPE

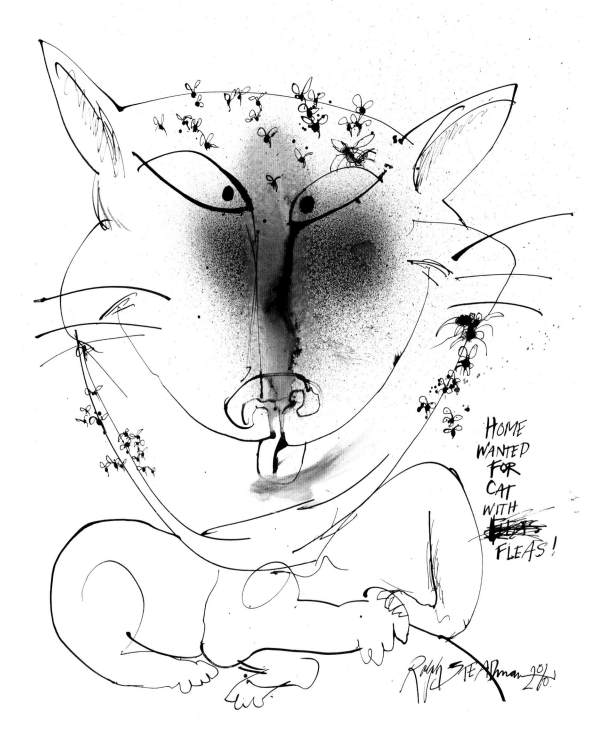

HOME
WANTED
FOR
CAT
WITH
~~FLEAS~~
FLEAS!

CATITUDE. Ralph STEADman 2070

CATS ARE ALL DIFFERENT—
BUT ALL VERY SIMILAR!

CHURCHILLIAN CAT

Ralph Steadman 2010

MANCATDOO

CATALYST of two Ralph STEADman 270

CAT AMONG THE PIGEONS— NOW WHAT??

Ralph STEADman 2010

CAT MESS

CATS KNOW SOME THINGS
BUT THEY DON'T KNOW
EVERYTHING

Ralph STEADman 2010

CANATOMY

Ralph STEADman 2010

BLAT

Ralph STEADman 2010

CAT LITTER

CAT LOVER
THERE'S ALWAYS
ONE !

Ralph STEADman

NICE PUSSY!

Ralph STEADman 2010

BAD CAT

Ralph STEADman 2010

THIS WAS A CAT — I'M NOT SO SURE.
IF IT'S NOT — THERE IS NO CURE.
DRAW SOMETHING ELSE ELSE
Ralph STEADman 2010

UNPLEASANT CAT

COMPASSIONATE
CAT WITH GAMMY LEG
AND INFECTION FROM MOUSE VICTIM

RECLING
NUDE
TWILLER

FAT CAT-2

Ralph STEADman 2010

SPLAT CAT WALK 5.

FRIENDS—Optional.

Ralph STEADman 2%

CATSPLAT WITH FRIEND 4   Ralph STEADman 2010

SPLATCAT 3. BROWN MACKEREL TORBIE - NO LESS! Ralph Steadman 2010.

SPLATCAT 1

I ONCE KNEW A CAT
IT'S AS SIMPLE AS THAT
WHEREVER IT SAT...
THAT WAS THAT.

NEWTON'S CAT
—THE REAL STORY!

SAMUEL JOHNSON'S CAT.